Building Your Knowledge

IN THE DIGITAL WORLD

By Megan Kopp

YOUR POSITIVE Digital Footprint

CRABTREE
PUBLISHING COMPANY
WWW.CRABTREEBOOKS.COM

Author: Megan Kopp

Series research and development: Reagan Miller

Editors: Janine Deschenes, Reagan Miller,

Proofreader and indexer: Angela Kaelberer

Design, photo research, and prepress:
Margaret Amy Salter

Print coordinator: Katherine Berti

Photo Credits

iStock: front cover, fstop123

Shutterstock: p 9 (middle left), tongcom photographer; p 19, (bottom right), Zull Must

All other images from Shutterstock

Library and Archives Canada Cataloguing in Publication

Kopp, Megan, author
Building your knowledge in the digital world / Megan Kopp.

(Your positive digital footprint)
Includes index.
Issued in print and electronic formats.
ISBN 978-0-7787-4588-4 (hardcover).--
ISBN 978-0-7787-4602-7 (softcover).--
ISBN 978-1-4271-2042-7 (HTML)

1. Internet research--Juvenile literature. 2. Research--Methodology--Juvenile literature. 3. Internet searching--Juvenile literature. 4. Electronic information resource searching--Juvenile literature. 5. Electronic information resources--Evaluation--Juvenile literature. I. Title.

ZA4228.K67 2018 j001.4'202854678 C2018-901257-9
s C2018-901258-7

Library of Congress Cataloging-in-Publication Data

CIP available at the Library of Congress

Crabtree Publishing Company

www.crabtreebooks.com 1-800-387-7650

Printed in the U.S.A./052018/BG20180327

 In Canada: We acknowledge the financial support of the Government of Canada through the Canada Book Fund for our publishing activities.

Published in Canada
Crabtree Publishing
616 Welland Ave.
St. Catharines, Ontario
L2M 5V6

Published in the United States
Crabtree Publishing
PMB 59051
350 Fifth Avenue, 59th Floor
New York, New York 10118

Published in the United Kingdom
Crabtree Publishing
Maritime House
Basin Road North, Hove
BN41 1WR

Published in Australia
Crabtree Publishing
3 Charles Street
Coburg North
VIC, 3058

Contents

Building Knowledge: Then and Now

Every time you gather facts for a school project or look up the batting average of your favorite baseball player, you are building your knowledge by searching for and accessing information. When you build knowledge you expand your understanding and viewpoint about a topic or idea. People build knowledge using different sources of information. How we access information and the types of **resources** available have changed over time.

Flashback to the Past

Decades ago, you had to travel to where the information was being held. You might go to a library. Most of the resources there would be in print form, such as books and newspapers. There might be films or audio recordings, too. Using a library card, you would check out materials you wanted to take home to read in more detail.

You build knowledge when you email an expert through an online forum or watch online videos to learn how to transform a pair of old jeans.

Flash Forward

Today, information comes to us. Thanks to devices that connect us to the Internet, such as smartphones, we can access resources anywhere—at home, at school, or out and about. Most libraries now have **digital collections** and ebooks. Technology has given us access to unlimited information sources by the pressing of a button.

Digital resources can come in different formats, including text, images, videos, and audio recordings. You can even take a **virtual field trip**, which lets you tour places around the world without stepping outside!

When you use digital technology, you are part of a community of digital users called **digital citizens**. Being a digital citizen can empower you to build your knowledge using a wide array of tools. You can also share the knowledge you build with the digital community. This book will help you answer big questions such as:

- Where should I look for information?
- How do I know if information is true?
- What tools and strategies should I use?

Becoming a Digital Citizen

As a digital citizen, you should always put safety first, respect the laws, and behave in a way that reflects how we would like others to treat us. Digital citizenship is also about learning how to use digital resources responsibly to build knowledge, answer questions, solve problems, and demonstrate your learning to others. In this book you will learn research strategies to help build knowledge using digital resources and tools. You will explore ways to use these skills at school and in your personal life.

A digital citizen:

- learns about the digital information sources available to them
- learns about new digital tools that support learning and uses them to build knowledge for school and personal interests
- learns how to choose the right tools for their needs
- builds knowledge to help find answers to questions and solve problems
- uses many different information sources to help make sure they understand all points of view
- shares their knowledge with others.

Every time you make a comment, send a message, post a photo, visit a website, use a **search engine**, or sign up for an app, you leave a digital trail online called your **digital footprint**. Being a good digital citizen means that you follow guidelines for safety online. But that is only one part of digital citizenship.

You will use digital tools all your life to gain knowledge. As a digital citizen, you can contribute to the digital community by sharing what you learn, along with your own ideas and creativity. This book gives you advice on how to choose the right platforms and tools to participate in the digital community.

DIGITAL DYNAMO

Curran Dee, Founder of DigCitKids

Curran Dee is eager to be a positive digital citizen. He understands how valuable digital resources can be. At the age of nine, Curran started a digitial citizenship website, http://www.digcitkids.com.

Curran's website encourages parents and kids to build knowledge and learn digital skills together. He also provides help for teachers and parents to learn about digital citizenship and digital literacy.

Ready, Set, Research

When you look for information on a topic, you are researching. It might seem easy to type a question into a search engine and receive an answer. But research requires active learning. As you research, you need to make connections between what you know about a topic and the new information you find. You also need to ask questions and consider new ideas.

The research process begins with a question. A good research question can't be answered with a simple "yes" or "no." After you ask your question, you find different sources of information about the subject. You have to interpret, or make sense of, the information. Then you can come up with a response to the question and share it with your peers.

Begin with a Question

Ask a question to begin your research. Remember that a good research question does not have a "yes" or "no" answer. Use some of these words to get started:

- How could ... ?
- What causes ... ?
- Why might ... ?

Look It Up!

A research question you might ask is, "What are people doing to save endangered tigers?" You will need to gather information from many different sources to answer it. Sources can be digital, print, audio, or from people who are experts on the topic. Knowing what resources are available and the benefits of each type will help you find the best resource for your needs.

How will you find your sources? In a study by Pew Research Center on how teens research in the digital world, 94% of teachers surveyed said their students are most likely to research using Google or other online search engines. A search engine searches the whole **World Wide Web** and can come up with a huge amount of information.

There are other ways to search the web, too. There are hundreds of online **databases**. These information sources are searchable and often include text from newspapers, journals, and magazine articles. Some databases are created for kids and include content at various reading levels.

Search Engine Strategies

Search engines are tools for finding content on the web. You might have used search engines such as Google, Bing, and Yahoo to build knowledge. Search engines gather information from millions of websites. They search web pages for the words that you type into the search bar, or source. A page of results will appear on the screen with **links** to web pages that have text matching your search words.

TECH TOOLBOX

True or False?

All search engines will list the same results.

This statement is false! Entering the same keywords into different search engines will not always lead to the same search results. That's because they access the World Wide Web differently.

Try it for yourself! Imagine you are looking for information about the question about endangered tigers on page 9. Type "endangered tigers" and "tiger protection" into Google. Then, type the same words into Yahoo. How are the results similar and different?

There are search engines for kids that show only age-appropriate results. KidzSearch.com and Kiddle.co are two examples.

Make Search Engines Work for You!

The question you type into the search bar directs all of the information that comes up—and therefore directs your research. The **keywords** you type are matched with words on websites all over the World Wide Web. Imagine how many results there are for common words, such as "dog" or "people."

Using effective keywords is a skill that takes practice. Often, the best keywords are found in your research question. They should reflect the central topic or topics in your research question. Descriptive keywords are best. It can be useful to delete words such as "of," "for," and "the."

Which keywords would you use to gather information about the question: "What are people doing to save endangered tigers?"

If you only get a few results or if you aren't finding the right information, try these tips:

- Use synonyms as keywords. For example, "save" might become "protect."
- Modify keywords so they are more specific. For example, "people" might become "biologists."
- Use quotation marks around keywords to make the search engine search only for the full word or phrase, exactly as you spelled it. That way, a search for "endangered tigers" won't show results about other endangered species.

Savvy Searching

Search engines return a huge number of results. Some sites do not have useful information. By using certain strategies, you can narrow down your online search results to only the most closely-related or useful sites. Choosing effective keywords when you search is one strategy. Another strategy is to use **Boolean operators**.

George Boole was a math whiz. He used three "key" words in his mathematical work. The words are "and," "or," and "not." Today, these same three words are called Boolean operators. These words are used to either narrow or expand your search results. Try each of the three searches shown below to discover how Boolean operators affect your search results.

Operator	Result
Using **AND** in your keywords tells the search engine to list sites that include **all** of the words you have entered.	**endangered AND tigers**: Only sites that contain **both** "endangered" and "tigers" will appear in your search results list.
Using **NOT** in your keywords tells the search engine to list sites that contain the word(s) you entered, **except** the word that follows NOT.	**tigers NOT endangered**: Any sites that contain the word "tigers" will appear in your results list, **except** those that also contain the word "endangered."
Using **OR** in your keywords tells the search engine to list results that contain **any** of the words you have entered.	**endangered OR tigers**: Any sites that contain **either** "endangered" or "tigers" will appear in your search results list.

In addition to keyword choice and Boolean operators, you can narrow your results by limiting your search to a specific format, such as only videos, images, news, or **scholarly articles**. Many search engines and databases have options for you to click your desired format.

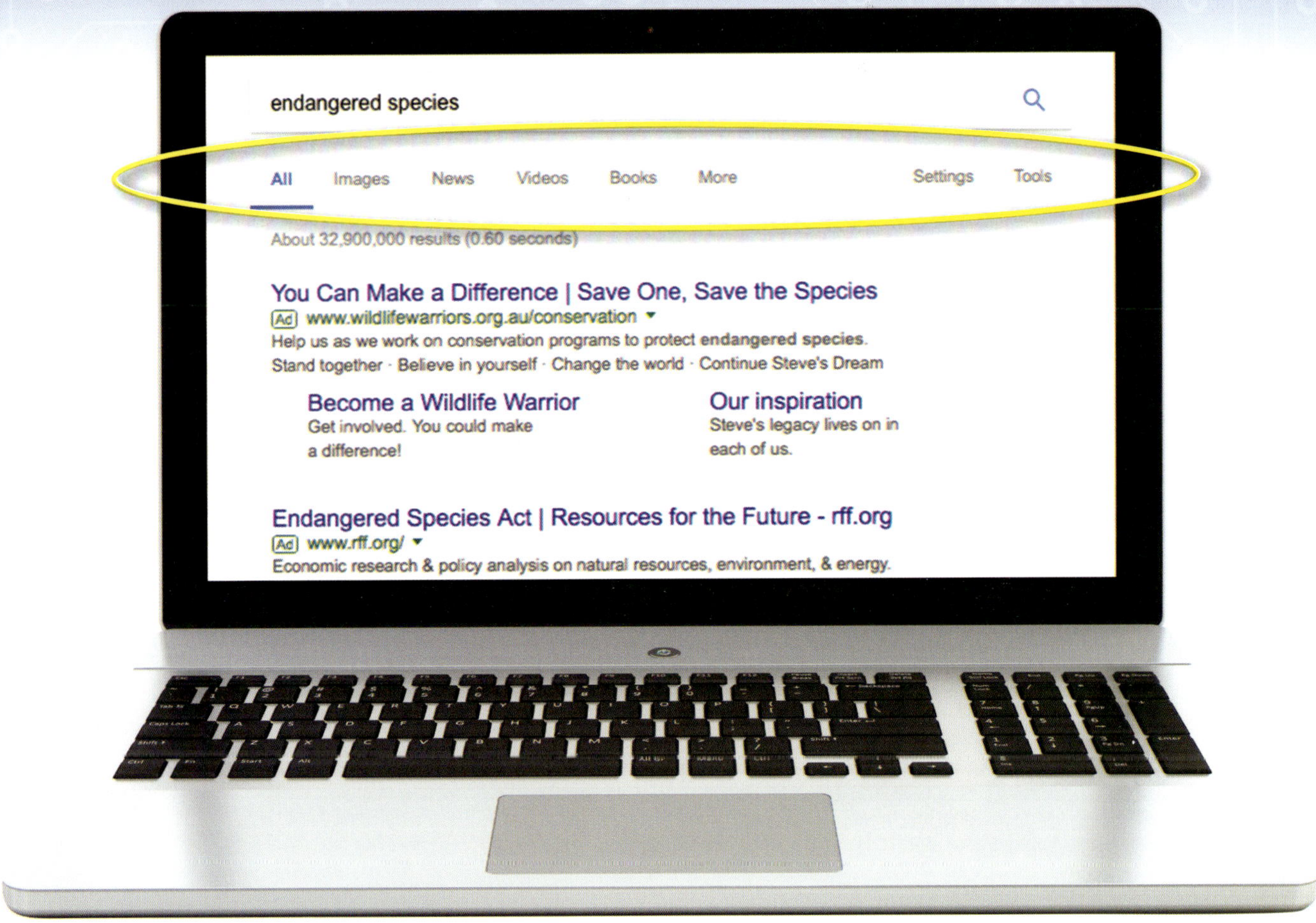

TECH TIP

Try using different domain suffixes to narrow your search!
All websites have a **URL**. This is a web address that leads directly to one site. The last three letters are called the domain suffix. The domain suffix points out the type of organization or geographical location.

.com = commercial or general purposes, e.g. Google's home search page, www.google.com
.gov = government, e.g. Library of Congress, www.loc.gov
.edu = educational institution, e.g. Smithsonian Learning Lab, https://learninglab.si.edu/
.org = organization, e.g. Common Sense Education, www.commonsense.org

Evaluating Sources

Not all content, or information, on the Internet is of the same quality. Books, magazines, and other print sources that you buy employ people to check facts and proofread materials. However, anyone with a computer can put content on the Internet. There is no requirement that free online content must be **evaluated**.

This is why it is important for you to evaluate content yourself. A good digital citizen always tries to use high-quality sources. A source is the place or organization from which you get information. To evaluate a source, ask yourself questions about its accuracy, credibility, relevance, and perspective.

ACCURACY:
Whether content is correct and without errors

ASK YOUSELF:

- Is the information on the site backed up with facts, **statistics**, or an expert quote?
- Does the site include a bibliography or links to the sources where it got the information?

BE CAREFUL IF YOU SEE:

- No facts, statistics, or quotes, or the site has not been updated for a long time

CREDIBILITY:

Whether the source is known for being reliable and believable

ASK YOURSELF:

- Who wrote the source? What is their training or education on the subject?
- Does the site's "About Us" section give information about the company, contacts, the backgrounds of staff, and FAQs?
- Is the URL from an organization, government, or education-based source? Is the site selling a product or service?

BE CAREFUL IF YOU SEE:

- No author names listed, spelling or grammar mistakes, disorganized information

RELEVANCE:

Whether the content is up to date and relates to the search topic

ASK YOURSELF:

- Does the information relate to my topic? Is it answering my questions?
- Is it well-organized and easy to navigate?
- Is the content written at my level?

BE CAREFUL IF YOU SEE:

- An old date or none at all on the information

PERSPECTIVE:

Whether the source has a specific belief or point of view that influences the way information is presented

ASK YOURSELF:

- Does the owner of the site represent a group, organization, or company?
- Do other sources on the topic have the same information?

BE CAREFUL IF YOU SEE:

- Writer sounds angry or uses name-calling, or presents only facts that support the writer's viewpoint

Believe It or Not!

There's a lot of discussion in the news and on social media about misinformation on the Internet. Misinformation is false information that is deliberately presented as true. Good digital citizens use and share information that is true or accurate. When you read information online, you have to judge whether it fits this **criteria**.

The good news is that there are strategies that can help you identify misinformation. Compare different sites on the same topic. Do they include the same or similar information? Check if the information is backed up by facts, statistics, or quotes by experts. Can you tell who the author of the site is and what training or education the author has? If the answer to these questions and statements is "no," you may need to learn more to judge whether the information is true.

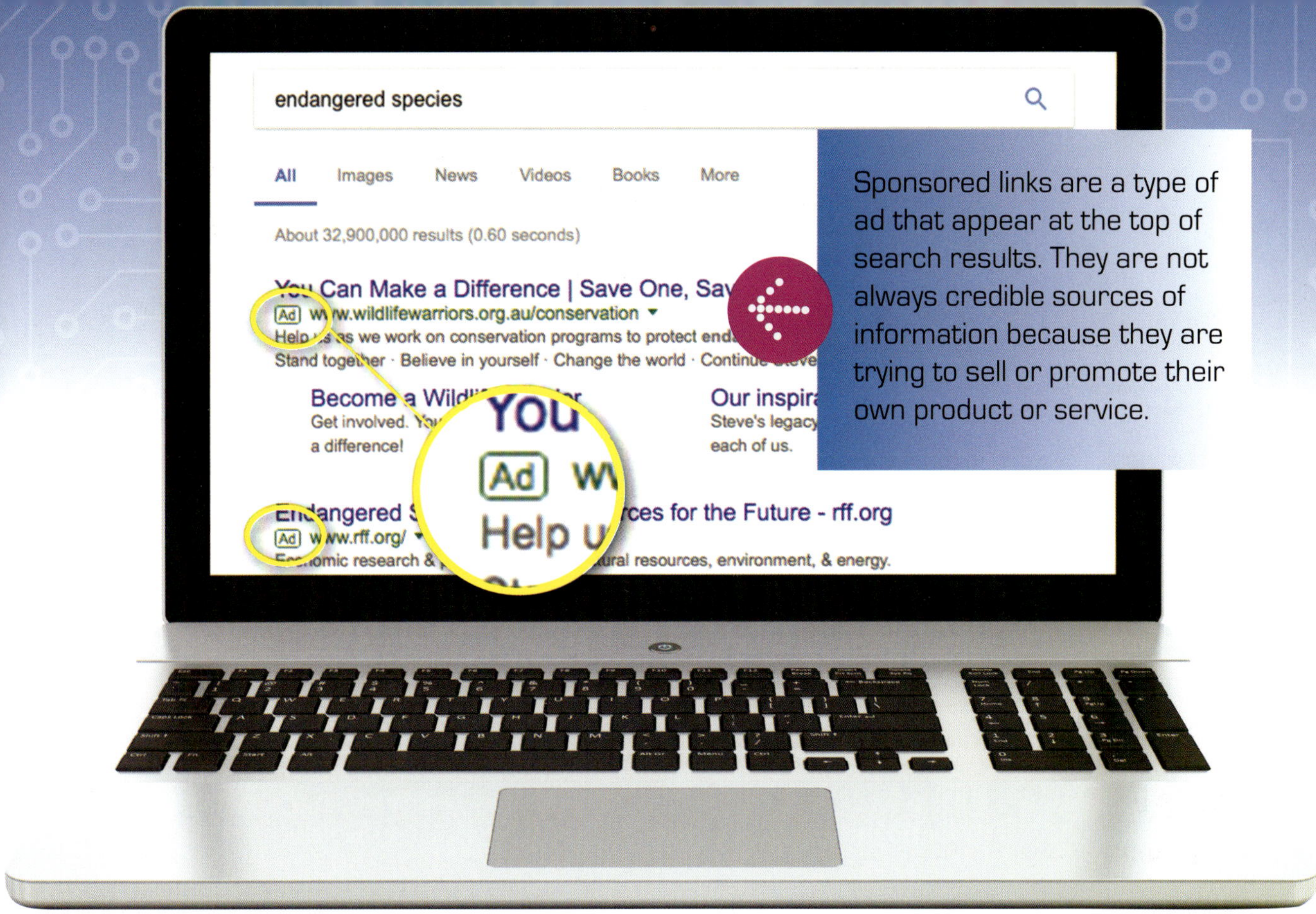

Sponsored links are a type of ad that appear at the top of search results. They are not always credible sources of information because they are trying to sell or promote their own product or service.

Can you pick out which of the sites listed below include fact-based information and which ones include misinformation? Review what you learned on pages 14 and 15 to evaluate each site based on its accuracy, credibility, relevance, and perspective. Give evidence to say why you think each site is accurate or not.

Fact-based or misinformation?

1. https://www.allaboutbirds.org
2. https://www.allaboutexplorers.com
3. http://www.funbrain.com
4. http://zapatopi.net/treeoctopus/
5. https://www.sciencenewsforstudents.org

Answers: Fact-Based Sites 1, 3, 5 Sites with misinformation 2, 4

Digital Distraction

Digital devices like computers, tablets, and smartphones are excellent tools for creating, collaborating, and connecting, but they can also be very distracting. If you don't learn how to concentrate and shut out distractions, you'll have a much harder time succeeding in building knowledge.

Tips to Avoid Distraction and Stay on Track

- *Before you begin, make a clear map of your questions and goals for what you want to learn. Ask yourself which questions you have answered, and for which you still need to find information.*
- *Focus on one part of your research at a time. It takes time and energy to redirect your attention from one task to another.*
- *Stay on track. There is a lot of interesting information out there and it is easy to get off-track. When looking at a source, ask yourself: "Does this site help me with my research?" and " Am I focusing on the most valuable information? "*
- *Learn how to close pop-up windows by clicking the X in the upper right corner. Don't be distracted by what the pop-up has to offer.*

QUESTION	INFORMATION I FOUND	SOURCE
How was the dishwasher invented?	- Josephine Garis Cochrane was the inventor - She wanted to find a way to wash dishes more quickly and safely than her servants could - In 1886, she built the first machine using a motor and wheel	kidsdiscover.com

Recording your Research

A great way to fight digital distraction is to record your research. Taking notes and recording your thinking helps to keep you focused on the question you want to answer. A graphic organizer, like the chart above, lets you keep track of the information you have found and its source. This allows you to see all of the information you have gathered in one place. You can print graphic organizers and write on them by hand, or type your notes into a digital notetaking program.

TECH TOOLBOX

Laser Focus

Notetaking apps such as Evernote, brainstorming tools such as Mindmeister, and bookmarks like those found on Google will help you record your research.

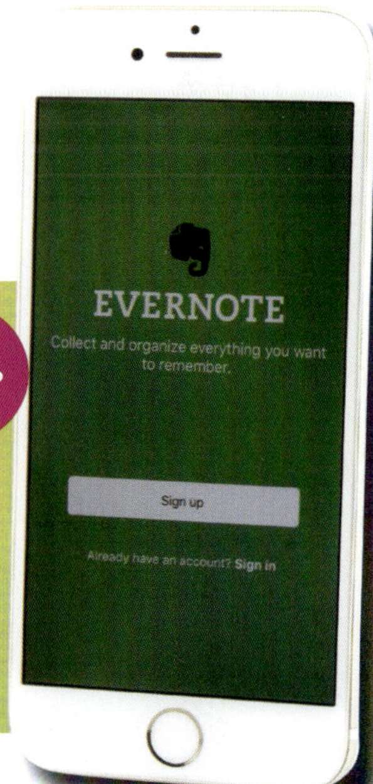

Giving Credit Where Credit is Due

Every time you write or create something, you own **copyright** to that creation. Copyright is a set of laws that protects your creative works. It means that only you have the right to make copies of this work and share it. It is against the law for someone else to use this material without your permission.

There is only one way to use someone else's work without getting their permission. You are allowed to use small portions of a work if you cite, or give credit to, the work's creator. This rule is called fair use. Fair use applies mostly to using portions of a work for education and research purposes. **Plagiarism** is the act of using the words or ideas of another person and claiming them as your own.

Copyright laws protect creative works in many different formats, including words, images, audio, and video recordings.

How to Cite a Source

Giving credit when using someone else's work is an important part of being a digital citizen. It is a sign of respect. It also helps support your research because people can find the sources you used and check that the information is correct. One way to give credit to someone else's work is to create a citation. A citation includes key information about a source, including the author's name, the work's title, its **publisher**, and its date of publication. The form to use for a citation depends on the type of information source used. Here is an example of a citation for an article found on a website:

● Author of article ● Article title ● Website title

Shaw, Allyson. "Top New Species for 2017." National Geographic Kids. National Geographic Society, 16 Dec. 2017. Web. 04 Jan. 2017. < https://kids.nationalgeographic.com/explore/nature/top-new-species-for-2017/>.

● Publisher ● Date the article was published ● Date you read the article online ● Website URL

DIGITAL DYNAMO

NICOLE, ASPIRING WRITER

Thirteen-year-old Nicole wanted to post her creative writing online to get helpful feedback from readers. She did research first to see which website would best protect her work from being claimed by other people as their own. Hear Nicole explain how copyright protects her work at this link: https://bit.ly/2qr3M91

Kids Can Curate!

Content curation is an important skill to help process the huge amounts of information at our fingertips. It involves finding, evaluating, organizing, and presenting digital resources that focus on a specific topic. The goal of content curation is to create a collection. A collection is a group of carefully-selected digital resources about your research question or topic of personal interest.

Content curators gather only the most useful, high-quality digital resources to build knowledge and share with others. The resources added to a collection are called **digital artifacts**. Artifacts may include links to websites, photographs, videos, or audio recordings.

Content curation is not about gathering as many resources as you can. It is about carefully evaluating resources to find those that best meet your needs.

Each artifact you include in your collection needs an **annotation**. An annotation includes information about the artifact, a short summary of the main ideas, and your reason for including it in your collection. Here is an example of an artifact annotation from an endangered tiger collection:

The source, or where it came from. Include the URL for web sources.

Name of the artifact

Date you accessed, or found, the source

"Bengal Tiger: What WWF is Doing"

https://www.worldwildlife.org/species/bengal-tiger

Accessed on April 4, 2018

This source is from the World Wildlife Fund (WWF). It gives information about the Bengal tiger and the challenges it faces as a species. It includes information about the current WWF effort to save the species, and what we can do to help.

Description of information on the source.

I think this source is useful because it comes from a organization that is recognized as being knowledgeable in the field. The source outlines real strategies that WWF is currently using to save Bengal tigers, so it helps to answer my research question.

Your reasoning for including the source in your collection.

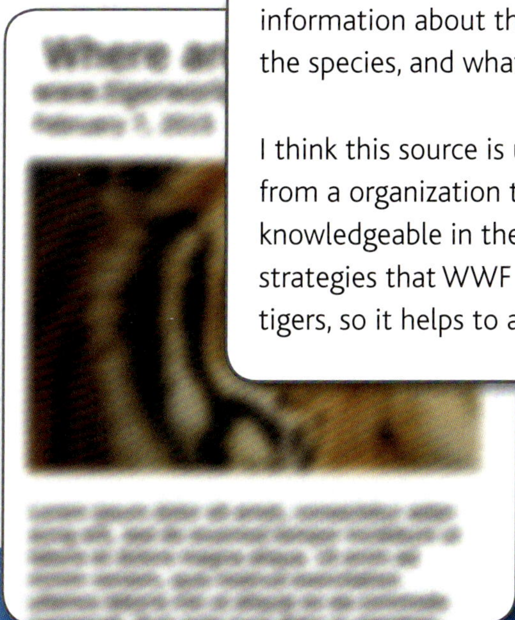

Collection versus Curation

As a content curator, you should have some goals for your collection. Your collection should have about 5-8 artifacts that:

- Cover all parts of your research question
- Have a variety of digital formats
- Come from credible organizations and individuals
- Represent different perspectives or points of view
- Use language you understand and is at the right level for your audience
- Represent current information and show how the information has changed over time
- Provide both a general overview of information and specific information about certain parts

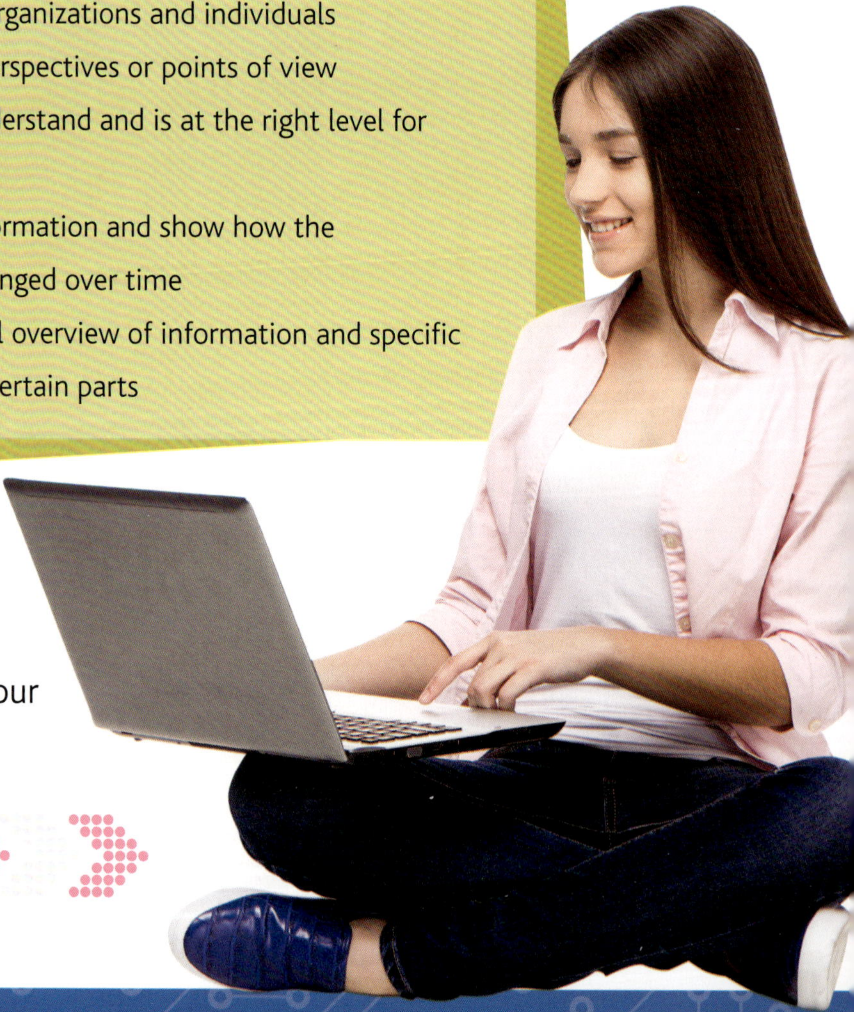

Use these criteria to guide your curation-building process.

Sharing Your Collection

Using content curation to create a collection is one way to showcase your knowledge about a topic. You can use your collection to support other projects on the topic, such as writing a report, creating a presentation, or designing an interactive poster. Sharing your collection can help others learn as well. Your carefully chosen artifacts provide a strong starting point for others to learn. You can share your collection with others through email, by posting it to your classroom or library website or wiki, or allowing others to access it online.

TECH TOOLBOX

Curation Tools

There are many websites and apps that can be used for content curation. Each is a tool that offers different ways to organize and present collections. The curation tools listed below have different rules for access. For example, you may need to create a free account using an email address to use a tool. Work with an adult to decide which tool is best for you.

1. **SymbalooEDU** (https://www.symbalooedu.com) Create collections of resource links presented as tiles on a grid.
2. **Diigo** (https://www.diigo.com/education) Post links to online resources and add comments using sticky notes.
3. **Sutori** (https://www.sutori.com) Add resource links to create interactive timelines and stories.
4. **LiveBinders** (http://www.livebinders.com) Organize resources using binders and tabs that can be private or shared.

Activity: Curate for a Cause

Sharing your collection can help raise awareness about an issue that you care about. It may encourage others to join in to solve a problem. For example, sharing a collection about endangered tigers could help make people aware of what still needs to be done to protect them.

You can curate and share collections that inform others about an issue at your school or in your community. Curate a collection that informs others about the issue below. You may also choose an issue that affects your school or community.

Issue: Our classroom creates too much waste from lunchtime.

Question: How can we encourage kids in our class to bring litterless lunches?

Collection goals:

The artifacts in our collection will:

1. Explain how litterless lunches help the environment
2. Show examples of litterless lunch programs at other schools
2. Give ideas for packing wrapper-free foods
3. Help us track our litterless lunch progress

Content Curation Tips

Think about these questions and tips as you curate your collection. You can also use the tips, strategies, and ideas you have read about in this book so far.

- What keywords will you choose to put into a search engine based on this question?
- What tools will you use to help keep track of the information you find?
- For each artifact, think about or describe to a friend the reason why you either kept or omitted it.
- What tools will you use to help share your answer with other people?

Share your collection with a friend or peer and ask them if they think the collection met your goals. Ask them if they have any suggestions to improve your collection. Then, reflect on your collection. Does it inform others about the issue or gather support to help fix it? Did it meet your goals?

Becoming a Lifelong Learner

Over time, you will continue to use digital tools to build and share your knowledge. You will search for and source credible, accurate, and relevant information as you move through school. You will also explore and expand your knowledge in the topics that interest you—in all areas of your life.

Digital citizens continue to build their knowledge throughout their lives. This includes building knowledge about the digital tools and strategies available to help you learn about topics that interest you at school and at home. As you try out more tools, you will discover the tools you like and the ones that work well for you. Over time, you will gather all of the tools you need to keep building your knowledge!

What tools do you use to explore your personal interests? Are there any tools you would like to try?

You Are in Charge!

The digital world changes rapidly. The way you receive information—and the format that information comes in—may be different in decades to come. New tools for accessing, analyzing, managing, evaluating, and communicating information come along regularly. All this means that digital citizenship requires the ongoing building of knowledge. The digital world is yours! Use it wisely and safely to build and share your knowledge to benefit others.

DIGITAL DYNAMO

TANMAY BAKSHI
TECH WHIZ AND TEACHER

Now 14, Tanmay Bakshi has been fascinated by computers since age five. At age nine, he launched his first app, tTables, which teaches multiplication.

Tanmay is passionate about sharing his knowledge. He coaches other kids in computer programming from his YouTube channel and has also written a book to teach others to create apps. Today, Tanmay works on creating artificial intelligence (AI) in partnership with the computer company IBM.

Glossary

annotation A description of a digital artifact, including the title and author, a summary of the main ideas, and an explanation of how the artifact helps build knowledge

Boolean operators Simple words used to combine or exclude keywords in a search

content curation The finding, evaluating, organizing, and presenting of digital resources that focus on a specific topic

copyright The exclusive legal right of a creator to print, publish, perform, or record material and to allow others to do the same

criteria The standards by which something may be judged or evaluated

critical thinking To ask questions, gather and analyze information, and make informed decisions

databases An organized collection of information; databases often include information not normally found online, such as articles from newspapers

digital artifact A digital resource included in a collection based on its high-quality and information value

digital citizen Member of a worldwide community linked by the Internet

digital collection An online database of digital resources about a topic, including text, images, audio, video, and other formats

digital footprint A record of a person's online activities

digital literacy The skills for using technology for different purposes, such as understanding and evaluating digital content

evaluated Judged or assessed based on criteria

keywords Terms used to search for information about a specific topic

links Codes that connect one part of a program with another. Links are often shown as bold, underlined, or colored text.

plagiarism The copying or making slight changes to some or all of someone else's work and claiming it as one's own work

publisher A person or company that prepares and sells digital or printed works

resources Tools or sources designed to help with a specific task

scholarly articles Research papers written by experts in a specific subject

search engine A program that searches for specific keywords on the World Wide Web

statistics Pieces of data taken from a research study or larger collection of data

URL The address of a web page

virtual field trip A guided online tour of a place or process

World Wide Web A connected computer network

Learning More

Books

Bodden, Valerie. *Using the Internet*. Creative Education, 2013.

Lindeen, Mary. *Smart Online Searching: Doing Digital Research*. Lerner Books, 2016.

Mason, Paul. *Understanding Computer Search and Research*. Heinemann Raintree Library, 2015.

Websites

http://www.21things4students.net/21/9-search-strategies/
This site offers guided learning challenges that reinforce digital skills, including online search strategies, website evaluation, and citing sources.

https://www.brainpop.com/games/searchshark/
This free online game provides a fun way for kids to practice identifying the best keywords to search for information on different topics.

https://learninglab.si.edu/
Smithsonian Learning Labs: This site allows users to curate digital collections using museum resources, including images, videos, text, and audio recordings. Users can gather, organize, describe, and share their curated collections with others.

Index

About the Author

Megan Kopp is the author of more than 80 nonfiction books for children and hundreds of magazine articles. She flexes her online creativity with a blog and through social media. She loves apps that help her track steps on the trail or teach her a language.